JAME

WHAT DO YOU WANT FOR CHRISTMAS?

An Advent Study for Adults

Abingdon Press | Nashville

For my family,
in celebration of all the great
Christmases we have shared

CONTENTS

WHAT DO YOU WANT FOR CHRISTMAS THIS YEAR?

I t happens every year. You can count on it. It always repeats itself. Again and again in the days leading up to Christmas, we will hear people ask the big question: "What do you want for Christmas this year?" Parents will ask their children. Husbands and wives, girlfriends and boyfriends will ask each other the time-honored question: "What do you want for Christmas this year?"

Usually, the question is asked and answered in a materialistic way: "What can I buy for you this year? a new toy? an item of clothing? a piece of jewelry? an electronic game or gadget?" But in this Advent study book, I want us to explore that question on a deeper level: What do we *really* want for Christmas? It's a fascinating thing to think about because Christmas has so many amazing and generous gifts to give us.

A few years ago, the Brookwood community in Brookshire, Texas, celebrated its twentieth anniversary. Brookwood is an amazing place, a modern-day miracle. It's a God-centered educational, residential, and entrepreneurial village for adults with functional disabilities. It's a special place for special adults. It enables them to grow, contribute, belong, and be productive. It gives them a place to live and a place to work in a safe community of love and acceptance and encouragement.

The Brookwood twentieth anniversary was quite a celebration. I was invited to have a little part in the big event. The guest speaker was Barbara Bush. In her talk, Mrs. Bush told a Christmas story about a little boy who wanted a red sled for Christmas. The boy sat down and wrote a letter to Santa, pleading his case. He wrote,

Dear Santa:

I really, really want a red sled for Christmas. If you will bring me a red sled, I will be a perfect little boy. I will be obedient. Whatever my parents ask me to do, I will do it immediately, if you bring me a red sled. Santa, I really do need a red sled.

The boy signed the letter and mailed it, but then he thought he needed a trump card—an insurance plan, a back-up strategy. So he went to the manger scene that his family had on display in their den. Secretly, when no one was looking, he reached over and picked up the figurine of Mary, took it upstairs to his room, and hid Mary in his closet.

The boy then went over to his bed, dropped down on his knees, and said, "Lord, I hate to get tough, but if you ever want to see your mother again, be sure that Santa brings me a red sled for Christmas!"

Now, I know there is a sermon there somewhere! I'm not certain what it is, but maybe it is this: even though the little boy was obviously confused about the real meaning of Christmas and even though he was far removed from the real spirit of Christmas, one thing is sure: he knew, with conviction, what he wanted for Christmas! Do *you* know with the certainty and the passion and the determination of that little boy what you want for Christmas?

I have thought about that a lot lately, and if I may be personal with you here at the outset, I would like to share with you my own version of what singer Natalie Cole calls "My Grown-Up Christmas List" in the hope that you will make a list of your own of the things you would like most for Christmas this year. Are you ready? Here is my list.

Put First Things First

That's what I want for Christmas—the good sense to put first things first.

Do you know what is the hardest thing about being a minister? It's not writing and preaching sermons. (That's the fun part for me.) It's not teaching or counseling or administrative details. It's not weddings or funerals. No, the hardest thing about being a minister is knowing how to use your time well; knowing when and where to put your weight down; knowing where you are needed most, where you can, at that moment, do the most good; knowing how to prioritize, how to "put first things first."

And you know, I suppose that is true in every profession. Doctors, lawyers, administrative assistants, teachers, scientists, engineers, architects, artists, entrepreneurs, whatever the profession, the question is the same: How do you use your time well?

It is also the hardest question for parents. Some of the most agonizing moments for us as parents have been those times when our job needed us and our family needed us at the same time. How do you decide? How do you choose? How do you balance it? How do you know how to put first things first?

We are all familiar with Reinhold Niebuhr's Serenity Prayer.

> God grant me the serenity
> to accept the things I cannot change;
> courage to change the things I can;
> and wisdom to know the difference.

We see that prayer everywhere—on plaques, on banners, on cards, on refrigerators. I wish we could create a similar prayer that would say something like this: "Lord, grant me the wisdom to know the important things in life and the will to do them first."

And when we stop to think about it, that is precisely the gift Christmas does give to us. Christmas, indeed, reminds us of the priorities. Christmas reminds us of the things that really matter: love, grace, faith, kindness, hope, trust, tenderness, truth, forgiveness.

Now, I don't know nearly as much about those good things as I would like to know, but what little I do know about them, I learned at church from the lessons of Christmas. So, that's what I put down first on my Christmas list of most-wanted items this year: the good sense to put first things first.

Always Be Gracious and Loving

Joey was very sad. It was just a few days until Christmas, and Joey was down in the dumps. His friend Tommy asked, "What's wrong, Joey? Why so sad?"

Joey answered, "It's Christmas, and I asked for a puppy, but my parents said no."

Tommy said, "That's no problem. You just have to come up with the right strategy."

"Strategy? What do you mean?" Joey asked.

"Well, it's really very simple," said Tommy. "If you really want a puppy, all you have to do is ask for a baby brother!" Two days later, Tommy saw Joey coming down the sidewalk, smiling broadly and holding a soft brown puppy in his arms!

Sometimes I think we go about things all wrong. We react too much and respond too little. We think of ourselves too much and of others too little. We trust power too much and love too little.

We think too much about what others will do for us and too little about what we can do for others.

I used to know a woman who was an insult collector. Some people collect stamps or rocks or matchboxes, but this woman collected insults. She always had a story to tell about somebody hurting her feelings. She was an insult collector.

Other people are grudge holders. Recently on an airplane, I heard a man say that if anybody ever does him wrong, they had better watch out, because sooner or later the opportunity would come for him to get 'em back. He was a grudge holder.

Wouldn't that be a terrible philosophy to live by? Well, Christmas teaches us not to be insult collectors, not to be grudge holders, but rather to be love givers.

This is beautifully illustrated in O. Henry's famous Christmas story "The Gift of the Magi," in which a husband and wife each sacrifice their prized possession for the sake of the other. The wife sells her beautiful hair to buy her husband a watch fob, while he sells his watch to buy her an expensive comb. Each gift then is materially useless, but the couple is exuberantly happy because they realize that each one's gift represents a gracious act of truly unselfish love.

It was *love* that came down at Christmas, not insults, not grudges, not pettiness, not hostility. Love came down at Christmas. What does that mean? Well, it means that God is love, and God wants us to be loving. God wants us to imitate his gracious ways.

That's what I want for Christmas: the good sense to put first things first and the Christlike spirit to always be gracious and loving.

Feel God's Presence in My Life

"No room in the inn"—that's the way the Scriptures put it. There is a heaviness, a pathos, a sadness about those words. That was the beginning of the Christ Child's life, and that experience would plague him for the remainder of his days on this earth: no room.

Harry Emerson Fosdick said it like this:

The crucial difficulty of Christ's life which denied him the service he longed to render, closed to him the hearts he longed to change and brought him at last to Calvary . . . was something so simple, so familiar, so little recognized as a tragic evil—so universal among us all, that one almost hesitates to name it— inhospitality.

That is the indictment on so many of us—our crowded lives slam the door in the face of the One we need more than anything.

There is a woman in our church who is a saint if I have ever known one. She has had a lot of heartaches and tragedies in her life. I have admired her so much because I have been to her home in times of great joy, and I have been there in times of great sorrow, and she is always the same: poised, serene, confident; she has that beautiful smile, that radiant, powerful expression on her face, that positive, hopeful attitude.

One day I asked her, "How do you do it?" And she answered, "Well, I have always had the feeling that no matter how difficult the experience is, God is with us."

God is with us. That is the message of Christmas; that is the promise of Christmas; that is the great gift of Christmas. God is with us, but we need to open the door and let him in.

What do you want for Christmas this year? I want the good sense to always put first things first, the good sense to always be gracious and loving, and the good sense to always feel God's presence in my life.

But we can't stop there because Christmas has so many life-changing gifts to give us. Love, joy, peace, hope, faith, salvation—these are some of the precious gifts of Christmas. But of course the best gift of Christmas, the one that makes all those other gifts possible, is the gift wrapped in heaven, God's gift of the Christ child. As Isaac Watts put it, "Joy to the world, the Lord is come!"

That's something to think about as we reflect together on the question "What do you want for Christmas this year?"

THE CHRISTMAS GIFT OF HOPE

Scripture:
Read Isaiah 6:8;
Luke 1:30-31, 34-35, 38

A friend of mine who is a psychologist once told me that he had found the perfect formula for getting through Christmas. He said, "You just put your mind in neutral and go where you are shoved!" Of course he was just kidding around, but we know full well what he was talking about. The Christmas rush, the hectic pace, the heavy traffic, the long lines, the frayed nerves, the bills, the deadlines, the pressures all combine to cause some people to give up and give in and just stonewall through the season. They just "put their minds in neutral" and "go where they are shoved."

But please don't let that happen to you. Don't just endure the season. *Enjoy* it. *Relish* it. *Savor* it. *Celebrate* it. *Learn* from it.

1

Share the joy of Christmas with others. Listen to what Christmas is saying; Christmas has so much to teach us.

Take Mary and Isaiah, for example. There is so much to learn from them. Isaiah lived in tough times. His people, the Israelites, were under attack, and they had gotten away from God—so far away that Isaiah knew that they needed a savior; that was the only hope now. Isaiah also knew that the people needed a prophet to call them back to covenant faith and to give them hope. He saw the need. He heard the call, and he responded, "Here am I, Lord; send me!" (Isaiah 6:8, adapted). Isaiah is the symbol for faith and hope.

We see it even more dramatically in Mary. Mary has so much to teach us about real faith and real hope. When we see her so beautifully portrayed in Christmas pageants and on Christmas cards and in Nativity scenes, she looks so serene and lovely, and the whole matter appears too simple and easy. But think realistically about it for a moment. Consider realistically what Mary, a not-yet-married young woman who had become pregnant, went through. It must have been incredibly difficult: the whisperings behind her back, the pointed fingers, the false accusations, the raised eyebrows, the questions, the gossip, the criticism, the family pressures, the crude jokes, the cruel laughter, the poverty, the heavy taxes.

Not even to mention the long, hard journey Mary and Joseph made to Bethlehem to register for the census, mandated at a time when an expectant mother shouldn't have had to travel anywhere except to the nearest hospital. Then add to that the birth in a stable, with no doctor, no midwife, no medicine, and no anesthetic—nothing but faith and hope in God!

Mary was just a teenage girl from a poor family who lived in an obscure village in a tiny nation, which itself was subject to a despised foreign power. Then one day, out of the blue, an angel came to Mary with a message from the Lord: "Do not be afraid, Mary, for you have found favor with God. And behold you will conceive and bear a son, and you shall call his name Jesus. He will be great. He will be the Messiah, the Son of God, the Savior of the world" (Luke 1:30-32, adapted). And all this was going to happen without Mary's ever having been with any man.

Now, be honest. Would you have believed that? The remarkable thing is that Mary did! That's real faith and real hope, isn't it? She was willing to hear God's word, obey God's will, and entrust the future into God's hands, even though it put her in an awkward, difficult, complicated situation. How would she explain this? How would she communicate this to her parents? How would she tell Joseph?

Mary and Joseph were legally engaged. They had not yet consummated their marriage, but they were considered "as good as married," and in those days, when you became formally engaged as they were, the only way you could be separated was through divorce. How could she tell Joseph that she was going to have a baby, and how would he handle it? And what would the neighbors say?

It was a tough situation for Mary, and under similar circumstances, most of us would have asked the Lord to find someone else to do this job. But not Mary. Her answer to the angel was a model of real faith and real hope. Like Isaiah before her, she said, "Here am I. I am the Lord's servant. Let it be with me according to your word" (Luke 1:38, paraphrased).

In both Mary and Isaiah, we see powerful portraits—Christian hope painted with three bold strokes. Let's look at these together.

Hearing God's Voice

Both Mary and Isaiah were tuned in to God. They were listening with the ears of faith and, thus, were able to hear God's message and respond.

I'm convinced that God is speaking loud and clear today, but sadly so few people are "tuned in" to hear him. So many of us get so caught up in the hectic pace of living that we stop listening. We are so inundated by words and voices and talk and appeals in our noisy world that we pull back into a hard shell and sleepwalk our way through life. Too many of us throw in the towel, retreat from the struggle, and give in to the sin of the closed mind. We don't want our world disturbed by new ideas, so we tune out. We have ears, but we will not listen and we do not hear.

There's a popular story that has been making the rounds. There may be some truth in it, while some of it may be legend. As the story goes, in the late 1800s, a conference of church leaders in Indiana held their annual conference on the campus of a local college. The president of that college addressed the assembled leaders, and he said, "I think we are living in such an exciting age. I think we are going to see things happen in our lifetime that right now are just unbelievable."

The presiding bishop was intrigued by the college president's remarks. The bishop interrupted him and said, "What do you see? What specifically are you talking about? What kind of new things do you mean?"

And the president of the college said, "Well, all kinds of things, Bishop. I believe we're coming into a time of great inventions. This is the year 1870, and I believe, for example, that one day soon we will be able to fly through the air like birds!"

"You what?" said the bishop. "You believe that one day we will be able to fly?"

"Yes sir, I do," said the college president.

And then the bishop expounded, "Why, that is heresy, sir. Just plain heresy. The Bible says that flight is reserved for the angels and the angels alone. Enough of that drivel. We will have no more such talk here. Flying! What a ridiculous idea!" And do you know what? When the conference was over, that same bishop, whose last name was Wright, went home to his wife and to his two small sons, whose names just happened to be Wilbur and Orville! The bishop had tuned out. He wasn't listening.

Now, put that over against this: some years ago, our family gathered in Memphis at Christmas for a family reunion. A month or so before Christmas that year, my sister had given birth to her third child, a beautiful baby girl. Most of us were seeing the baby for the first time, so there was a lot of excitement about this new addition to our family.

Toward evening, we put the bassinet in the back bedroom of the house and put the baby to bed. All the travel and excitement had tired her out. She fell asleep almost immediately. We had our Christmas dinner, and afterward, we exchanged gifts. Then people got involved in a variety of activities. Some were talking and visiting, others were playing electronic games, some were singing carols, and still others were watching a football game on television.

There was a lot of noise and happy Christmas confusion. In the midst of all the chaos, I noticed my sister quietly slip out of the room. Where do you think she was going? She was going to check on the baby. She had heard the baby cry out.

Isn't that something? In all the commotion, no one else heard the baby, but the baby's mother did. And you know why, don't you? Because she was tuned in to hear the baby. She was listening for the baby. Her ears were trained to hear her baby's cry. That was her number one priority.

In the same way, Mary was tuned in to hear God. Listen! One of the great questions of Christmas is this one: Can you hear the baby?

Are you tuned in to hear God?

Above all the chaos, can you hear God? Is that a priority for you?

Or have you closed your mind and shut the voice of God out of your life?

Mary's hope and Isaiah's hope were great, first of all, because they heard God's voice.

Obeying God's Will

In the original New Testament Greek, the word for faith is *pistis*, and it literally means "believing obedience," believing in God so much that we commit ourselves body, mind, and soul to the doing of God's will, come what may.

In one *Peanuts* cartoon, Linus, the statistician for Charlie Brown's baseball team, brings Charlie Brown his final report. "I've compiled the statistics on our baseball team for this last season," Linus says. "In 12 games, we ALMOST scored a run. In 9 games, the other team ALMOST didn't score before the first out. In right field, Lucy ALMOST caught 3 balls, and she once ALMOST made the right play." And then Linus says, "Charlie Brown, we led the league in ALMOST!"

That's the way many people are with regard to obeying God's will. They "lead the league in almost." They almost obey God's will, but not quite.

Many years ago, when the great missionary David Livingstone was serving in Africa, he sent an appeal to England for more workers to come help him with his mission work on that continent. An answer came back from England, "We would like to send more workers to help you, but first we must ask, is there a good road to the outpost?" David Livingstone wrote back these words: "If you are offering to send workers who will come only if the road is easy, I can't use them. Tell them to stay home."

Mary's hope and Isaiah's hope were not tentative or conditional. No, in both cases, it was total and complete obedience to God, no matter how rough the road may be. Mary's hope and Isaiah's hope were great because they heard God's voice and because they obeyed God's will.

Trusting God's Power

Both Mary and Isaiah took things one step at a time, one day at a time, and trusted God for the future.

Some years ago, there was a captain on a Mississippi riverboat. He had been on that job for more than thirty-five years. One day a passenger said to him, "After all these years of navigating the river, I guess you know by now where all the rocks and sandbars are." The captain answered, "No, but I know where the deep water is!"

In effect, that's what Mary said, isn't it? "I know where the deep water is." In other words, I know there are some rocky places out there, but I trust God to bring me through this.

I heard Terry Anderson say that a few years ago. He had just been released after having been held hostage for six and a half years in another country. He was serving as the chief Middle East correspondent for the Associated Press when he was kidnapped in Beirut, Lebanon, on March 16, 1985, and he was held captive until his release on December 4, 1991. It was an incredibly difficult ordeal, but Terry Anderson came through it all with amazing strength.

Since his release, he has been interviewed a number of times, and his answers and responses have been inspirational. Let me remind you of three of his most powerful comments. First, when he was asked what had enabled him to survive this awful experience, he answered without hesitation, "My companions, . . . my faith, [and my] stubbornness," which might be seen as another way of saying trust in God.[1]

Second, one reporter said, "Terry, you have said that you don't hate your captors. Can you help us to understand that?" Terry Anderson replied, "I don't hate anybody. I'm a Christian . . . and it's really required of me that I forgive, no matter how hard that may be, and I intend to do that."[2]

And third, he was asked, "Terry, did you ever lose hope?" Terry Anderson said, "Hard question. . . . Of course, I had some blue moments, moments of despair, but fortunately, right after I became a hostage, one of the first things that fell into my hands was a Bible. Over the last six and a half years as a captive, I have spent a lot of time with the Bible . . . and that helped me so much because it's about hope; it's about trust in God, and that's what gave me the strength to make it through each day." And then

Terry Anderson said, "You do what you have to do. Faith helps you to do what you have to do. I spent a lot of time with the Bible and it reminded me to do the best I could each day...and to trust God for the future."

That's great Christian hope, isn't it? It's the kind of hope Mary and Isaiah had. It's the kind of hope we need—Christian hope that enables us to hear God's voice, to obey God's will, and to trust God's power.

Questions for Reflection and Discussion

1. What does Advent mean to you? Why is it important?
2. What are some of the lessons and learning opportunities Christmas brings to us?
3. What are some different ways in which we hear the voice of God?
4. What does it mean to be a person of great hope? What personal traits and qualities does a person of hope possess?
5. What lessons about hope can we learn from the lives of Mary and Isaiah?
6. God wants us to both trust and obey; is this difficult to do? Explain your answer. Share some ideas on how we can be more trusting and obedient.

Prayer

Dear God, thank you for the season of Advent. Help us grow in hope and faith as we move toward Christmas. Show us how to celebrate and enjoy this special time of year, and guide us in observing the true meaning of Christmas. Amen.

Focus for the Week

Begin your observance of Advent by becoming an instrument of faith and hope to others this week. Through words and actions, reach out to those in need.

THE CHRISTMAS GIFT OF FREEDOM

Scripture:
Read Matthew 11:1-6

Some years ago there came out of Southern California a poignant story that is a powerful parable for Advent and Christmas.

A twelve-year-old boy had been brought to the hospital. He had been thrown off of a horse. The boy was so traumatized by that frightening experience that he had become the victim of an emotional paralysis. He was paralyzed in a prison of fear. His eyes were open, but he stared straight ahead. He made no recognition of anyone else, and he would not move or speak. He would make no response to anyone or to anything.

The doctors said there was nothing physically wrong with him—no bruises or cuts or broken bones, no concussion. The diagnosis was that he had been literally "scared stiff," frightened into some kind of psychosomatic paralysis. Day after day, the boy lay in bed in that kind of semiconscious state of mind and spirit, totally unresponsive. Nothing reached him.

Finally, one day in a moment of inspiration, one of the nurses brought in a baby, a happy six-month-old baby. The nurse laid the baby on the stomach of the twelve-year-old boy. The baby started cooing and scratching the little boy's stomach. Then, the baby crawled up and began to touch the little boy's face.

Suddenly, the twelve-year-old boy smiled, and then he hugged the baby and patted him and kissed him on the top of his head. Amazingly, that twelve-year-old boy had come back to life. He began to talk and respond and recognize, and in just a few days, the doctors pronounced that he was well, and they let him go home. Isn't that something?

This story underscores the incredible message of Advent and Christmas. A little baby comes to set us free. A little baby comes to heal us, to save us, to give us new life. A little baby comes to do for us what no one else can do. Advent reminds us of how much we need a Savior. And Christmas tells us the good news: a Savior is given!

One of the most popular passages of the Advent season is this colorful story in Matthew 11. John the Baptist sends his disciples out to ask Jesus a question: "Are you the one who is to come, or are we to wait for another?" (verse 3). Now, this is a curt question. What we have here is a situation where two cousins are going at each other! And we can understand John's impatience. He is in prison.

A short time before, he had rebuked King Herod publicly. Herod had stolen his own brother's wife, and John the Baptist, in his typical hard-hitting, prophetic style, had publicly reprimanded the king. He had exposed King Herod's sordid, selfish, sinful ways. King Herod didn't like that, so he took his revenge. He arrested John the Baptist and threw him into the dungeons of Machaerus, a fortress in the mountains near the Dead Sea.

Here in prison, John the Baptist begins to get a bit impatient with his cousin Jesus. John sends his disciples out to Jesus with this question: "Look! Are you the one who is to come, or shall we look for another?" What John is asking Jesus is this: "What are you waiting for? You have the power. When are you going to rally the people and lead the march on Rome? When are you going to get with the program? When are you going to get this kingdom going? When are you going to smash the Romans and seize the throne?"

But look at how Jesus answers: "Go and tell John what you hear and see: the blind receive their sight, the lame walk, the lepers are cleansed, the deaf hear, the dead are raised, and the poor have good news brought to them" (Matthew 11:4-5). Now, what did Jesus mean by that? Simply this: Jesus meant that he had chosen not the way of might or power or wrath but the way of love. Jesus had chosen to bring the Kingdom with love because he knew that love is the most powerful thing in the world, the most lasting thing in this world.

It is love that sets us free, and that's what Jesus was saying to his cousin. "Look, John, at what's happening. Can't you see it? People are being set free, and that's what the Kingdom is about. The blind receive their sight, the lame walk, lepers are cleansed. Love came down at Christmas (in a Christ Child) to set people free from those things that imprison them."

That's *still* the good news of Christmas. The Christ Child can set us free from those awful things that shackle us and paralyze us and rob us of the zest of life. The love of the Christ Child is still strong enough to bring us out of those prisons and give us a new lease on life. Let me show you what I mean.

The Prison of Selfishness

He tells us to come out of that prison, and he teaches us how to be loving and self-giving. Indeed, Jesus' teachings against selfishness are almost startling. Listen to his words:

Those who want to save their life will lose it, and those who lose their life for my sake will find it.

(Matthew 16:25)

What will it profit them if they gain the whole world but forfeit their life?

(Matthew 16:26)

*I give you a new commandment, that you love one another. Just as
I have loved you, you also should love one another.*

(John 13:34)

*If any want to become my followers, let them deny themselves and
take up their cross and follow me.*

(Matthew 16:24)

You see, in effect, Jesus is saying, "Come on out! The doors are
open! You don't have to live in the prison of selfishness anymore."

Some time ago, an article appeared in *The Columbus Dispatch*
that makes the point dramatically. It shows graphically what
love—real love—is all about. The article tells the story of a man
who is terminally ill and lying in a hospital bed, his wife beside
him. The man, although being given the best medical care, is in
a great deal of pain. With a weak voice, he tells his wife that he is
thirsty, and she gently helps him take a sip of water as she lovingly
places an arm around his shoulders and mops his forehead with
a cool, damp cloth. With this scene as the backdrop, the article
writer makes this observation:

> So in the end love comes down to this . . . not some Clark Gable
> appraisal of Vivien Leigh or some sex symbol's seductive pose,
> but "Help me sit up." In the end love is not a smoldering glance
> across the dance floor, the clink of crystal, a leisurely picnic
> spread upon summer's clover. It's the squeeze of a hand. I'm
> here. I'll be here no matter how long the struggle. I'm in it
> for the duration. Water? You need water? Here. Drink. Let me
> straighten your pillow.[3]

That's what real love is.

Now, let me ask you something. Do you know love like that? Do you love anybody like that? You can't live in the prison of selfishness and love like that. The Christ Child came into the world to set us free from the prison of selfishness, from the sin of selfishness, and to show us the real meaning of love, the real meaning of sacrificial, self-giving love. He showed us in a manger. He showed us with his healing touch. He showed us on a cross that love—not selfishness—is the way God meant for life to be lived.

That's the first thing to notice here. Christ can free us from the prison of selfishness.

The Prison of Hate

I don't know of anything more dangerous and destructive to our spiritual lives than hate. Hate will absolutely poison your soul. Listen! If you feel hatred right now toward anyone, for that person's sake, for your sake, for God's sake, get rid of that! Turn that over to God and let God cleanse you right now before it's too late.

Some of us grew up with the great comedy team Abbott and Costello, and many more are probably familiar with their classic "Who's on first?" routine. One night on their radio program, Lou Costello was wearing a beautiful flower in his lapel. People kept complimenting his lapel flower, much to Costello's delight.

However, a neighbor named Scott came along, admired the flower, and then suddenly, without warning, Scott pulled the flower out of Costello's lapel, put it on himself, and walked away whistling. This made Lou Costello very angry, and as the program went on, Costello got madder and madder at Scott for taking his flower.

Finally, after replacing his lapel flower with another one, Lou Costello said to Bud Abbott, "I'm ready for Scott now. Just let him try to take my flower out of my lapel now and see what he gets!"

"What have you done, Lou?" asked Bud Abbott.

Lou Costello answered, "I have put a hand grenade in my coat pocket, and I have tied the flower to the pin of that hand grenade. When Scott takes my flower this time, it's gonna blow his hand clean off. *That'll* teach him!"

Now, let me hurry to say that no one should try such a thing at home; the radio days of Abbott and Costello were very different times, and a comedy routine like that, while done tongue-in-cheek, probably wouldn't go over the same way today. But it does help to demonstrate one very important point. You see, what Lou Costello didn't realize was that while the trap he was setting would do harm to his neighbor, at the same time, it would blow his own heart right out! That's the way hate works. When we lash out at others in hatred, we blow our own hearts out.

Jesus knew that, and that's why he came preaching love and mercy and compassion and forgiveness. And that's why he exposed hatred as a terrible and destructive enemy of real life.

There's no question about it: hate is a terrible prison to live in. But the good news of Christmas is that Christ can set us free. Love came down at Christmas to bring goodwill to all people and to set us free from selfishness and hate.

The Prison of Unconcern

Jesus said, "Go and tell John what you hear and see: the blind receive their sight, the lame walk, the lepers are cleansed, the deaf hear, the dead are raised, and the poor have good news brought to them" (Matthew 11:4-5). Christ came to show us how concerned God is, how much God cares, how deeply God loves, and he sends us out into the world so that we may love and care and serve other people in that same self-giving way.

Some weeks ago, I saw something that fascinated me. As I was driving to church, I saw a young woman out for her morning walk. All of a sudden, a huge dog came over a fence (barking and growling and snarling), and the dog charged right toward the young woman. Now, what do you think the young woman did? Run away? Climb a tree? Jump into my car? Scream for help? No, none of these! Rather, she ran straight at the dog. She challenged him! She stared him down! She turned him back! She ran him off! And then she continued her morning walk.

Now, what was it that made her so courageous? Let me tell you: it was love! It was love! For, you see, she was not alone that morning. Her baby was with her. She was pushing her baby in a stroller. And when the barking, snarling dog started toward them, that woman did what any mother would do. She positioned herself between the dog and her baby. She was more concerned about her baby's safety than her own! She was more concerned about her baby's welfare than her own! Her love set her free to care, to be concerned, and to be courageous.

That's the love of a mother. But let me tell you something: it is also the love of a Christian! That's the kind of concern we are supposed to have for all of God's children.

The Christ Child comes at Christmas to set us free from the prisons of selfishness and hate and unconcern, but we, in faith, have to decide to walk out the door!

Questions for Reflection and Discussion

1. Advent reminds us of how much we need a savior. How does the arrival of the Christ Child minister to us and to others?

2. Reread Matthew 11:2-6. How did Jesus respond to the question of John the Baptist—"Are you the one who is to come, or are we to wait for another?" What did Jesus mean by his answer?

3. Share a time when you were in a prison of selfishness. How did you escape?

4. How can we gain freedom from the prison of hate?

5. What are some of the causes and cures for unconcern?

6. What are some ways you can give the gift of love or freedom this Christmas?

Prayer

Dear God, thank you for setting us free through the birth, death, and resurrection of Jesus. Show us how to escape from the prisons that hold us back from loving others and that keep us from doing your will. May this Advent be a time of reflection and growth for us all. Amen.

Focus for the Week

If you could wrap up the gift of freedom, who would you give it to, and why? How can you help give others the gift of freedom this Christmas season?

THE CHRISTMAS GIFT OF CHRIST

Scripture: Read Luke 2:15-20

Several years ago, Thomas Sutherland spoke at an event in our community. His schedule was so hectic at the time that the organizers of the event had to schedule his speech for 7:00 in the morning. Fifteen hundred people turned out at 7:00 a.m. to hear him speak. Tom Sutherland: Do you recognize that name? Let me refresh your memory.

Tom Sutherland had been a prisoner and had just been released. While serving as Dean of Agriculture at the American University of Beirut in Lebanon, he had been taken captive near his Beirut home by members of a terrorist group and had been held in captivity for more than six years, spending a significant amount of that time in solitary confinement. In his speech to our community, he said something I will never forget. He said, "Do

25

you know what it's like to be in prison? to be held hostage? to be a captive? It's very lonely, and you worry that people will forget you. I felt abandoned. I didn't think anybody even knew I was in prison."

During his time of imprisonment, Tom Sutherland could hear a radio that the guards had. It was tuned into the BBC channel, and every day Tom Sutherland would listen intently to the newscast, hoping and praying that he might hear his name, hoping and praying that the newscaster would talk about him on the air and tell the story of his imprisonment and his innocence. But his name was never mentioned, so he assumed that no one in the United States even knew that he was being held hostage.

Finally, after more than six years of captivity, Tom Sutherland was released. The United States government flew Tom's wife, Jean, to his location so the two could be reunited. They were so excited to see each other. A few days later, they flew home together to San Francisco. As they were getting off the plane back home in the United States, Tom Sutherland was amazed to see that there were lights and television cameras, reporters and people holding signs, and a huge crowd at the airport. Tom turned to his wife and said, "Jean, look at all these people. There must be a celebrity on the plane with us! Look around and see if you can spot who it is." And Jean said, "Honey, they are all here for you! It's you! This is all for you!"

When his wife told him that, Tom Sutherland started crying, and he couldn't stop. He sobbed like a little boy. He couldn't believe it. He said, "I thought everybody had forgotten about me. I didn't think anybody knew I was in captivity. I felt completely abandoned. I didn't think anybody cared. Thank God I was wrong."

The shepherds at the first Christmas must have felt something like that. Society had cast them out and pushed them down to one of the lowest rungs on the social ladder. They were considered unclean physically and spiritually, and they must have felt abandoned and forgotten. They must have felt as though no one really cared about them. But then they found out on that first Christmas night that, thank God, they were wrong. Somebody *did* care! The One who counts the most did care! He was there for them! Of all the people on the face of the earth, the angel of the Lord appeared to them. And as they made their way to Bethlehem to see the miracle of Christmas, they discovered in the process three great gifts that Christmas gives to us, three great gifts that money can't buy, three great gifts available now to you and me. Let's take a look at these together.

Acceptance through Christ

The shepherds found the gift of acceptance.

In December of 1993, in an awards ceremony held in my community, the Paul "Bear" Bryant Award for coach of the year was presented to Terry Bowden, who was in his first year as the football coach at Auburn University. Terry Bowden had taken a struggling program that was on probation and had led his team to an undefeated season. It's interesting to note that Terry Bowden's father, Bobby Bowden, who is the coach at Florida State, was also nominated for the award. There was a lot of good-natured joking and teasing at the awards banquet about this father and son being considered for the same prestigious award. And of course, when the son, Terry Bowden, won, no one in the room was happier or prouder than his father.

In his acceptance speech, Terry Bowden thanked his team, his fellow coaches, Auburn University, and then he thanked his family.

"I owe so much to my parents," he said. "Many of you in this room know my mother, and you know how special she is, but let me tell you about my father. My parents always took us five kids to church. Even when we were on a trip, they took us to church. Once while on vacation, we went to this church that was a little more emotional than we were used to. The minister was shouting and pounding the pulpit, and he began to look around the congregation for someone to single out, and he spotted my father. Mom and Dad had marched us down to the front pew. Mom was on one end, Dad on the other end, with the five kids squeezed in between to be sure we would behave in church. The preacher pointed dramatically to my dad and this conversation took place.

"You there. Do you have faith?"

"Yes, I have faith," Dad answered.

The preacher said, "If I put a two-by-four board down there on the floor, do you have enough faith to walk across it?"

"Yes, I could do that."

"But," said the preacher, "what if I took that same two-by-four board and placed it across the top of the two tallest buildings in New York City. Would you have enough faith to walk across it then?"

"No, I don't have that much faith," Dad answered.

"But what if somebody were standing on the other end," said the preacher, "and dangling one of your children off the side. Would you cross the board then?"

Terry Bowden said that at this point, his father turned and looked down the pew at his five children, and then asked the preacher, "Which one?"

Now, of course, Terry Bowden was just kidding around, because the Bowdens are a very close-knit, loving family. But the point I want to make is this: our Father, God, does not say, "Which one?" He doesn't say, "Which one should I lay my life on the line for?" God so loved the world that he wants to bring us all into the circle.

God comes with the open arms of acceptance for all of us. To each one of us, he says, "You are valued. You are included. You are wanted. You are precious to me. This is for you."

Now we have to do our part. We have to accept his acceptance. We have to receive this gracious gift. We have to welcome him into our hearts and lives with faith; but this Christmas present of acceptance is offered to us from God, and when we receive it and live in that spirit and pass that gift on to others, then we are giving them a Christmas present wrapped in heaven—the gift of acceptance.

If you want to give something special to someone at Christmas this year—to your children, your parents, your neighbors, your coworkers, your friends—just say to them, "You are valued, you are included, you are wanted and needed. You are precious to me." However you want to say it, express that, and you will be giving them a Christmas present—the gift of acceptance.

Forgiveness through Christ

Steven Spielberg's movie *Schindler's List* is a graphic, shocking, unflinching depiction of the twentieth century's most staggering horror: the methodical, brutal extermination of millions of human beings in the Nazi death camps of World War II. Oskar Schindler was a most unlikely hero, but through the efforts of this one man, nearly twelve hundred persons were saved from certain death. He put them to work in his factory, where he could protect them.

One of the most powerful moments in the movie is when Oskar Schindler is in conversation with the commander of the labor camp in Kraków, Poland. They are talking about power, and the commander (in his swaggering way) brags about the authority he has over these people. A man comes before him, and he has the absolute authority to kill that man, to exterminate that man, if he so chooses—and the commander has been in the habit of doing just that, brutally killing people right and left, with no conscience at all. But Oskar Schindler says, in effect, "Oh no, Commander, you are wrong. That is not power. Anyone could do that. But to have a man come before you and to say, 'I could take your life if I so choose, but no…instead I pardon you! I pardon you!' That, Commander, is power!" It is indeed the power of forgiveness, and that's the Christmas gift God offers us.

Martin Luther once became so frustrated with the evil he saw going on around him that he shouted, "If I were God, and the world had treated me as it treated Him, I would kick the wretched thing to pieces." Luther might have done so, but not so with God. God comes into the world offering the gift of forgiveness: "I pardon you. I forgive you. I want to reclaim you." That's the gift God offers, but we have to do our part. We have to accept the gift in faith. And when we accept forgiveness and offer forgiveness to others and live in the spirit of forgiveness, then we are doing a God-like thing. We are offering a Christmas present wrapped in heaven, the gift of forgiveness.

There is the gift of acceptance and the gift of forgiveness.

The Gift of Christ

That's really what it's all about, isn't it? Several years ago, our grandson Paul, who was four-and-a-half years old at the time, said to his mother, "Mama, I love Christmas almost as much as I love you." Paul's mother said, "Well, tell me, Paul, what you love about Christmas." And Paul answered, "I love the lights. I love the presents. And Mom, there's one more thing, and you are going to like this best: most of all, I love the baby Jesus."

Paul was right. His mother did like that best, because she has taught Paul and his sister that Jesus is the reason for the season. Indeed so! Jesus is God's gift to the world, the gift of the Savior, a gift that money can't buy.

We received a Christmas card once that expressed it well. The message read like this:

> Socrates taught for forty years, Plato for fifty, Aristotle for forty, and Jesus for only three.
>
> Yet the influence of Christ's three-year ministry infinitely transcends the impact left by the combined 130 years of teaching of these greatest philosophers of all antiquity.
>
> Jesus painted no pictures, yet the finest painting of Raphael, Michelangelo, and Leonardo da Vinci received their inspiration from Him.
>
> Jesus wrote no poetry, but Dante, Milton, and scores of the world's greatest poets were inspired by Him.
>
> Jesus composed no music; still Haydn, Handel, Beethoven, Bach, and Mendelssohn reached their highest perfection of melody in the hymns, symphonies, and oratorios they composed in his praise.

Every sphere of human greatness has been enriched by this humble carpenter of Nazareth.

Precisely! No question about it: The gift of Christ is the best Christmas gift of all. Patrick Henry understood that, and he expressed it in the way he closed his will. He said, "I have now disposed of all my property to my family. There is one more thing I wish I could give them, and that is the Christian religion. If they had that and I had not given them one shilling, they would have been rich; and if they had not that, and I had given them all the world, they would be poor."

Remember at the start of this chapter how Tom Sutherland thought he had been forgotten and that no one cared? Remember how, when his plane landed in San Francisco, he saw all of the people and the lights and the cameras, and he thought there was a celebrity on board the plane, and his wife said to him, "It's you! This is all for you"? Well, that's what I want to say to you about Christmas: *It's all for you!* The Christmas gift of acceptance, the Christmas gift of forgiveness, and the Christmas gift of Christ— they are all for you!

Questions for Reflection and Discussion

1. What parallels are there between the shepherds in the fields on that first Christmas and the story of Tom Sutherland?

2. Share a time when you were given the gift of acceptance. How did it feel?

3. How do you receive the gift of forgiveness? How do you give it to others?

4. Give some reasons why the gift of Christ is the greatest gift of all.

5. What qualities are found in a "perfect" gift? What makes a gift valuable or treasured?

6. How do you give the Christmas gift of Christ to others?

Prayer

Dear God, thank you for the gift of Christ and for the joy your gift brings to us and to others. Help us share Jesus with those who need to know the real joy and meaning of Christmas. Amen.

Focus for the Week

On behalf of Christ, be a giver of special Christmas gifts this week. It could be sharing the gift of a smile, going out of your way to help someone, listening to someone who needs to talk, or finding some unique way you can minister to others.

THE CHRISTMAS GIFT OF SALVATION

Scripture:
Read Luke 2:1-7

Have you heard about the little boy who loved going to church? He enjoyed the music, the Scriptures, the creeds, the sermon, and the fellowship. The only part about going to church that the little boy didn't like were those long pastoral prayers! He really liked his minister, but the minister prayed such long pastoral prayers, and sometimes it seemed to the little boy that the prayer would never end.

Then one Sunday, the little boy's parents invited the minister home for Sunday lunch, and, would you believe it, the boy's mother asked the minister to pray the prayer of thanksgiving before the meal. *Oh, no!* thought the little boy. *We will never get to eat. I'm starving, and he will pray forever.* But to the boy's surprise, the minister's prayer was brief and to the point. The minister prayed, "O Lord, bless this home. Bless this food, and use us in your service. In Jesus' name. Amen."

The little boy was so astonished by the minister's short prayer that he couldn't help himself. He looked at the minister and blurted out what he was thinking: "Man, you don't mess around when you're hungry!"

Well, I don't want to "mess around" in this fourth week of Advent, just before Christmas, because I know that whether we realize it or not, we are hungry. We are all hungry for God. We are all hungry for our Savior. We are all hungry for Christmas, because, you see, this is precisely what Christmas is all about. We need a Savior, we are starved for a Savior, and a Savior is given!

The name *Jesus* literally means "the Lord is salvation" or "Yahweh saves" or "Savior." Jesus came at Christmas to do for us what we cannot do for ourselves. He came to save us from our sins.

Some years ago a young woman named Karen became a missionary. She was a well-trained nurse and was sent to serve in a Methodist mission hospital in a remote corner of Africa. Karen loved her work. She knew that God had called her to this special healing ministry, and she felt incredible fulfillment in bringing much-needed love and medical care to the people in this impoverished region of the world.

But as Christmas approached, Karen's thoughts turned toward home. Christmas had always been a wonderful time for her family. They would always go to church together on Christmas Eve and then open presents together on Christmas morning. What could she send them? She wouldn't be able to go home for Christmas that year, so she would send her presents by mail; but what to send? She had very little money and no place to shop, and mailing a bunch of large presents was out of the question.

Then Karen smiled; she knew just what to do. Some days later, a small box arrived at the front door of her parents' home. When Karen's mother found the box and saw the postmark from Africa, she knew it contained Christmas presents from Karen. On the outside of the box, written in bold print, were these words: "Please open on Christmas morning with the whole family." So on Christmas morning, after all of the other presents had been exchanged, Karen's mother opened the box. Inside it, she found a number of envelopes—one for Karen's father, one for her mother, one for Karen's sister, one for her brother-in-law, one for her niece, and one for her nephew. When the family members opened the envelopes, at first they were surprised. Each envelope held a small piece of poster paper. The pieces had been cut into funny shapes. Suddenly, they realized it was a homemade jigsaw puzzle, and each family member had one piece of the puzzle. Quickly, they went to a table and put the pieces together, and when the last piece was put into place, they realized that the puzzle they had put together was in the shape of a heart. On the homemade poster paper heart were inscribed these words from Karen:

Silver and gold have I none,

But such as I have,

I give to you.

I give you my heart.

This is what God did for us on that first Christmas: God sent us his heart! He sent his only son into the world to save us, to redeem us, and to turn our lives around. God sent us his heart to show us how much he loves us and to show us how he wants us to love one another.

God sent his only son into the world to be our Savior, but what does he save us from? Of course, he saves us from our sins. But let me mention also three other things he saves us from.

Saving Us from Disillusionment

Outside of the Bible, the most famous Christmas story ever written is *A Christmas Carol* by Charles Dickens. What can you remember about that story? Well, most everybody knows that Charles Dickens's story is about a gruff, miserly character named Ebenezer Scrooge. We probably also recall that there is a little boy in the story named Tiny Tim Cratchit, who (the opposite of Scrooge) is most always happy and is always saying, "God bless us, every one!"

Now, we remember that much about the story. But actually, if we look closer, we see that this is a story about conversion—and, oh my, did Scrooge ever need converting! I mean, he was a despicable character—a selfish, arrogant, greedy, hard-hearted, mean-spirited, uncaring, unsympathetic, unchristian tightwad. Scrooge's now-famous response to Christmas—"Bah! Humbug!"—has become the sad symbol of such disillusioned spirit.

As the story unfolds, Ebenezer Scrooge is visited one night by some ghosts who subject him to a haunting the likes of which few characters in fiction have experienced. Scared out of his wits by the ghosts, Scrooge is forced to see himself as he really is. The visits of the ghosts, and the Christlike, unconditional love of the Cratchit family, who keep on loving him even though he has treated them horribly—those two things combine to convert Ebenezer Scrooge.

And now with a second chance, he changes completely! A skinflint no more, Scrooge becomes instead an ever-loving grandfatherly type. He *loves* Christmas now. He gets into a loving spirit of the season, sending presents to the Cratchits and a large amount of money to charity. He dresses up and goes to his nephew's house for Christmas dinner and announces to his clerk, Bob Cratchit, that he will be receiving a nice raise. Talk about a conversion! Talk about a life redeemed and saved! Here we see a life turned around!

Why are we so fascinated with this story? It's not just that it's a well-written classic piece of literature. There is something more here. The truth is, this is *our* story. Deep down inside, deeper even than some of us realize, we all relate to Ebenezer Scrooge! That is to say, we all need help; we all have unknown flaws; we all need to

41

face up to ourselves; we all need to be converted from selfishness to love. Or to put it more dramatically, we all need a savior!

Well, this is the good news we celebrate at Christmas. Two thousand years ago, God looked down and saw the sick, disillusioned, Scrooge-like spirit of the world, and God knew that would not work, so he sent his son to save us and to change us and to show us a better way. Christ came to change us from greedy, selfish, disillusioned people into generous, loving, gracious servant people.

That's number one: Christ saves us from disillusionment.

Saving Us from Defeat

In 1939, a man named Robert L. May worked in the publicity department for Montgomery Ward stores. He was asked, for publicity and marketing purposes, to come up with a new story for Christmas. May mixed two stories, the story of Santa Claus and the story of the Ugly Duckling, and he created this new story called "Rudolph the Red-Nosed Reindeer."

The Rudolph story quickly caught on, and over the next couple of years, Montgomery Ward distributed more than six million coloring books telling the story of Rudolph, the red-nosed reindeer. Robert May's story of Rudolph became so popular that ten years later, in 1949, Mr. May's brother-in-law, Johnny Marks, wrote a song about it. Gene Autry recorded the song, and, as they say, the rest is history.

You know why we like the Rudolph story so much, don't you? It's not just because it's a cute, child-friendly story, not just because the song has neat words and a catchy tune. No, we like this story because it's about rising above defeat. It's about turning an difference into an advantage. It's about turning a defeat into a victory.

You may remember that early on, like the Ugly Duckling before him, Rudolph was despised and rejected and teased and taunted because of his red nose. But then, in the end, with outside help, he becomes the hero. He saves the day with his "nose so bright."

Now, let me remind you of another Rudolph—Wilma Rudolph. In the summer of 1960, I was glued to my TV, along with millions of other Americans, to watch one of the greatest athletes of all time perform in the Olympic games. She was a tall, long-legged young woman from Clarksville, Tennessee, representing the United States.

When the 1960 Summer Olympic Games were over, Wilma Rudolph had become the first American woman ever to win three gold medals in track and field, and along the way she set both an Olympic and a world record. It was a remarkable achievement, even more amazing than you might think, because, you see, as a small child, Wilma Rudolph had battled polio (as well as bouts of pneumonia and scarlet fever), and her left leg was severely affected. The doctors were not encouraging at all. They told Wilma's family that she would never be able to walk without the aid of heavy braces.

But Wilma Rudolph's mother refused to accept that diagnosis. In her daily prayers, she asked God to bring strength to Wilma's weak legs, and she began massaging and exercising Wilma's legs when Wilma was four years old, determined to help her little girl walk. Wilma's mother trained the older brothers and sisters on how to massage and exercise Wilma's weak left leg. Four times a day for almost five years, the family members took turns working with little Wilma, and more times than that every day, they prayed for her. Finally, Wilma got better and got a brace for her leg, and then she progressed to a heavy high-top shoe. One day, when Wilma was about eleven years old, her mother looked outside to see her daughter running and jumping and playing basketball, and Wilma was barefooted—no brace, no custom shoe!

Wilma Rudolph went on to become the fastest woman in the world because she and her family refused to quit when life dealt them a hard blow. They were people of faith, and they refused to accept defeat.

Remember that powerful verse in Paul's letter to the Philippians: "I can do all things through [Christ] who strengthens me" (Philippians 4:13). I like the way my seminary professor paraphrased this message. He said that it means, "Bring it on! I'm ready for anything, for Christ is my strength."

When Christ came into the world as a baby born in a stable, he came to a world where many people felt down-and-out and defeated. He came to show them and us that he will be with us always, and that he can lift us above anything that threatens to defeat us. He showed us in a manger and he showed us on the cross that his love is the most powerful thing in the world and that if we believe in him and trust him, nothing can defeat us. Christmas comes around once each year to remind us of that. Christ can save us from disillusionment. He can save us from defeat.

Saving Us from Death

The Scriptures remind us that nothing—nothing, not even death—can separate us from the love of God in Christ Jesus our Lord (Romans 8:39).

My friend Jim Harnish was the pastor of Hyde Park United Methodist Church in Tampa, Florida. In one of his books, Jim told a story about a member of his staff, Vee Choate. Jim Harnish called Vee "a first-class joy-bringer." She could light up a room.

As Jim said,

Vee loved Christmas! Vee knew how to keep Christmas well! She did it with the same military order and precision that she employed as our church's wedding coordinator to get bridesmaids to stand up straight, groomsmen to spit out their chewing gum, and wedding photographers to obey the church's rules. Every box of her Christmas decorations was numbered and labeled. She even kept photographs of the decorations so that she could begin with an accurate record of how things had been done the year before. It took a full week but by Thanksgiving each year, her home, her office, her wardrobe—I suspect, even her dogs—had become the objects of her Advent transformation.

As Jim said, Vee kept Christmas with beauty and grace and love. She kept Christmas by giving gifts and by throwing a big party and by making music. She did it all and made it look so easy. When people thought of Vee, the word that came immediately to mind was *celebration*: "She celebrated life and love and friendship, and she invited all the rest of us to join in the celebration." Continuing, Jim said,

> Beneath it all, Vee knew how to keep Christmas because she knew that the Christ who was born in Bethlehem had been born within her life. The result was that the love and grace of God that became flesh in Bethlehem became flesh among us in our relationship with her.

But then on December 10, 2001, Vee died in a car accident—so full of life, so full of Christmas, and then so suddenly gone. At her memorial service, Jim Harnish said, "Some of us might be tempted to say that Christmas will be almost unbearable because of Vee's death. But the deeper truth is that Vee's death would be unbearable were it not for Christmas."

A year later, Vee's husband wrote a devotional for the church's Advent booklet, and in it he said, "On December 10, 2001, the biggest joy in my life was snuffed out." As Jim Harnish said,

> [Vee's husband] described the way he struggled to find out how to face Christmas without her. He began asking what God and Vee would have him to do. Then the answer came: Do what we've always done. Go back to church. Sing in the Messiah. Attend your Bible study class. Stay close to friends and family.

And don't forget to decorate the house (with at least two trees). Looking back, he said, "By doing what I believe she and God wanted me to do, I found I could still sing 'Joy to the World' and be thrilled by the 'Hallelujah' chorus. . . . The nights are still lonely, and some days are longer than others, but I have been able to find joy."[4]

Do you know that kind of joy? It's the joy that comes from knowing Christ as our Lord and Savior and from knowing that, come what may, Christ will be with us and will deliver us, because he has the power to save us from disillusionment, from defeat, and even from death.

Charles Wesley said it all when he put it like this:

Hark! the herald angels sing, "Glory to the newborn King;"

. . . .

Mild he lays his glory by,
born that we no more may die,
born to raise us from the earth,
born to give us second birth.[5]

Questions for Reflection and Discussion

1. What are some ways in which God satisfies our hunger at Christmastime?

2. What is the best Christmas gift you ever gave or received? What made this gift so special and treasured?

3. What is disillusionment, and what are some of its causes? How can people be saved from disillusionment?

4. Share a time when God helped you rise above defeat or turn a defeat into a victory.

5. What friends or relatives who have passed away do you remember at Christmastime, and what special memories of them come to mind?

6. When you think of the Christmas gift of salvation, what images or thoughts come to mind?

Prayer

Dear God, thank you for the many gifts of Christmas, especially the gift of salvation. Help us celebrate this special time of the year by sharing the love of Christ with others. Open our eyes to the joys of this season and to the needs of others. Amen.

Focus for the Week

Christmas will be here soon. Spend some time reading the Christmas story and reflecting upon it, and ask yourself the question, "What do I *really* want for Christmas this year?" Focus this week on the spirit of the season, the real meaning of Christmas. Share the good news of God's precious gift of the Christ Child with others.

NOTES

1   Chris Hedges, "The Last U.S. Hostage; Anderson, Last U.S. Hostage, Is Freed by Captors in Beirut," *New York Times*, December 5, 1991, https://www.nytimes.com/1991/12/05/world/the-last-us-hostage-anderson-last-us-hostage-is-freed-by-captors-in-beirut.html.

2   Stephen Kinzer, "Anderson Says He Doesn't Hate Captors," *New York Times*, December 7, 1991. https://www.nytimes.com/1991/12/07/world/anderson-says-he-doesn-t-hate-captors.html.

3   Mike Harden, "When Love Goes Beyond Romance," *Chicago Tribune*, April 3, 1988, https://www.chicagotribune.com/1988/04/03/when-love-goes-beyond-romance/. Thanks to Norman Neaves for this illustration.

4   James A. Harnish, *All I Want for Christmas: An Advent Study for Adults* (Nashville: Abingdon Press, 2003), 33–36.

5   "Hark! the Herald Angels Sing" (lyrics, Charles Wesley, 1739; alt. by George Whitfield, 1753, and others), *The United Methodist Hymnal* (Nashville: The United Methodist Publishing House, 1989), #240.

Made in United States
Orlando, FL
03 November 2025

71896694R10036